For Jill

CONTENTS

INTRODUCTION

Several boxes of writing samples followed me like an old hound dog from New Jersey to Texas. These boxes held the original papers written by tenth graders for the 1977–1979 New Jersey Writing Project tests, the first holistic scoring partnered by Educational Testing Service in Princeton, New Jersey, Rutgers University, and a consortium of disparate school districts across the state of New Jersey.

Every so often I'd pat that old hound dog, remembering that era of my academic life, thinking *these might come in handy some day.* But when the twentieth century rolled into the twenty-first, I purged boxes and papers during the ritual called "the cleaning of the garage" and put the old hound dog to sleep.

Still, like the hoarders on those horrid TV shows, the parting was wrenching. Me, sitting cross-legged on cold cement going through the boxes like the end of a jazz routine or "Mack the Knife"—playing it one more time.

What I discovered underscores the thesis of this book and my personal mantra, "If you teach it, they will learn."

Writing by those kids in 1977 was embryonic, stilted, formulaic. Of course there were stars—children of Princeton professors or of Bell Lab scientists—but for the vast number of students not yet exposed to much writing or to writing as a process, kids who had no voice (didn't even know what voice was in writing) or who had suffered through humiliations connected with their papers returned hemorrhaging with red ink or who had experienced pressure akin to water-boarding until they read their papers aloud in front of the entire class, those kids contented themselves with an anorexic paragraph or two; they obviously never re-read, never considered mentor texts, never did prewriting, or any other part of the process for that matter.

As teachers, we rejoiced if they filled a page when we taught them. We agonized over the kids who wrote nothing—we cajoled and bribed them, pleaded, and sometimes even wrote parts for them, and on good days, we inspired them.

That's what these decades-old papers told me because I couldn't help juxtaposing them in my mind with writing I see today— confident writing replete with voice and conviction, coherent interesting writing that beckons the reader to read on, risk-taking writing with syntactic touches of genius.

What happened during those thirty-some intervening years? Teachers happened. Teachers who began writing themselves, teachers who took additional courses in writing and extended training in writing, teachers who joined writing groups and who began to publish, teachers who read about writing and wrote about reading. Teachers who were excited enough about the process to transmit that excitement to their students. That's what happened—they taught, not assigned, writing, and kids learned and loved the learning.

But the reflexive writing generating most of that excitement was personal narratives—both teachers and students explored themselves, their texts, their worlds. Now we have been challenged to turn our attention, our zeal, and our knowledge to persuasive writing.

This book will provide the theory and strategies to help that happen. Remember: "If you teach it, they will learn."

CHAPTER

1

FOUR
HISTORICAL
INFLUENCES ON
PERSUASION

> The purpose of these studies is to raise problems, not to solve them; to draw attention to the field of inquiry, rather than to survey it fully; and to provoke discussion rather than to serve as a systematic treatise.
>
> —Stephen Toulmin

As with all things significant, looking, however briefly, at the history of persuasion gives the present state of teaching it a context. Here we offer a thumbnail sketch of the four major influences in rhetoric, which "is defined by Aristotle as the art of finding in any given subject matter the available means of persuasion" (Joseph, 227). We have framed this history less as theory and more as method. These four influences are the Greeks, the Romans, thinkers of the nineteenth and twentieth centuries, and present-day commentary.

I. THE GREEKS

The Greeks codified persuasion but called it "rhetoric." They studied it, used it in their courts, and applied it in their city-states.

Plato

While some in the classical tradition considered persuasion the art of eloquent expression, Plato regarded it as the art of rational discourse —a philosophical search for truth. When we think about Plato, we think truth.

Here's how a Platonian thesis would read:

> *Neutered dogs escape cancer of the reproductive tract.*

Based on scientific evidence—hence rational thought—Plato would have stated the truth as known—neutered dogs escape a certain type of cancer. Plato believed in persuading based on truth.

Aristotle

Aristotle insisted that while rational discourse should be enough to persuade someone, he believed that "It is not sufficient to know what one ought to say, but one must also know how to say it" (*Rhetoric Book III*, 1403b). He thought words were morally neutral, but the intent for good or ill determined how they were used.

Aristotle believed persuasion was accomplished through *logos*, appealing to the minds of the audience by proving the truth of the thesis; *pathos*, putting the audience in the right frame of mind and emotion to favorably receive the information; and *ethos*, inspiring the audience through good intention, confidence, and high moral character. When we think of Aristotle, we think intent.

Here's how Aristotelian theses would read:

People should neuter their dogs.

or

People should not neuter their dogs.

Because Aristotle believed in the moral neutrality of words, he would want the thesis to be clear in terms of the rhetorical stance.

The Sophists

Meanwhile, the Sophists held that the art of persuasion resided in the means—*any* means—even those that deceived or manipulated people, even those untruthful, exaggerated, dishonest, or fallacious. Lacking moral purpose, they did not concern themselves with mastering the art of persuasion, rather they used rhetorical sleight-of-hand and ambiguities to achieve their goals. When we think of the Sophists, we think of the desire for power: they epitomize the adage, "language is power."

Here's how a Sophistic thesis would read:

Poor, bedraggled dogs don't need to bring more sick dogs into this world.

Often using language to manipulate the audience—in this case arousing feelings of pity for dogs—Sophists used any means to make their point. Truth was not an issue; they wanted power.

Aristotle attempted to reconcile these rival factions by formulating a fully developed theory that claimed eloquence and truth (factual evidence) as persuasion's essence.

II. THE ROMANS

We have the Romans and their adaptation of Aristotle's conception of rhetoric to thank for our Western tradition of rhetoric. Considered the art of the popular, Romans used persuasion in law, politics, ceremonies, and religious events. Because it was oral and open to debate, they concentrated on the probable, not the conclusive.

Cicero

The Roman rhetoricians further shaped Aristotle's theory of persuasion. Cicero, the great orator, in his treatise *De Inventione* (84 B.C.), introduced the notion of probability versus demonstrated truth when he said "Invention is the discovery of valid or seemingly valid arguments to render one's cause probable." With that statement, Cicero defined the first of the five canons of persuasion: invention, arrangement, style, memory, and delivery. When we think of Cicero, we think probability.

Cicero would frame his thesis:

Neutered dogs make life easier.

The word *probably* hangs over this statement because the word *easier* is open to interpretation. What might be easier for one person might not be easier for another—yet the probability of ease due to neutering is implied.

Probability enters into almost every law case in modern times. How many times do we hear, "Beyond a reasonable doubt . . . ?"

Quintilian

Quintilian added the notion of credibility to persuasion: the good man must speak well—to persuade, a person had to possess high moral character and be knowledgeable to be credible. Hence criminals hire lawyers and lawyers coach their clients on how to put forth their best "face." When we think of Quintilian, we think credibility.

Here's how a Quintilian thesis would read:

The American Veterinary Medical Association contends neutered dogs develop fewer tumors.

Clearly this thesis establishes a high degree of credibility by referencing the AVMA. Unless the opposition had equal credibility, this would be difficult to refute.

These theories dominated rhetoric until the beginning of the nine-teenth century, when changing ideas about people and life influenced and shaped philosophy, rhetoric, and logic.

III. THINKERS OF THE NINETEENTH AND TWENTIETH CENTURIES

Three things impacted classical rhetoric. First, the growth of science and technology demanded expository writing, writing that conveyed information. Second, the rise of the middle class brought along its insecurity about language and its desire to educate everyone. Third, ideas changed about what makes us who we are.

Ivan Pavlov

In a nutshell Ivan Pavlov with his theory of conditioned stimulus led persuasion to absorb a certain amount of stimulus-response. His theory dismissed man as a rational animal and promoted the notion that certain responses condition people. Not unlike dogs, ring the bell and we salivate. Therefore, according to Pavlovians if you offer the right reward, you'll convince people. Likewise, if you punish, you may convince people, too. One is positive conditioning; the other negative conditioning. Right or wrong, reward or punishment con-vinces. When we think Pavlov, we think conditioning.

Here's an example of a Pavlovian thesis:

Neutered dogs learn faster.

While Plato would have a problem with the truth of this thesis, Pav-lovians see it as an example of training. To them it's all a matter of rewards and punishments, either/or, conditioned response.

Sigmund Freud

Sigmund Freud's theory of psychoanalysis gave us the rhetoric of per-suading through knowledge of prior experiences or unconscious mo-tivations. When we think about Freud, we think of the unconscious.

Freud might say:

Neutering dogs curbs their instincts.

Freud believed the unconscious drives humans; he further believed that anxiety is one of those strong drives. To convince people they should neuter their dogs, Freudians would prevail upon that unconscious drive of anxiety to persuade because a dog not neutered causes its owner anxiety.

Carl Rogers

Carl Rogers, on the other hand, moved psychoanalysis to psychotherapy with his "Nineteen Propositions," which provided the basis for his two major theories: the actualized person and positive reinforcement. For persuasion, his idea was to strip the person of feelings of threat so he or she could consider alternatives based on a true self. When we think of Rogers, we think self-realization.
Here's a Rogerian thesis:

To ensure a contented dog, it should be neutered.

Rogers believed in the "force of life" as a way for all living creatures to actualize or achieve full potential. For dogs to be fully healthy and do the best they can, he would make the case for neutering them.

Kenneth Burke

Kenneth Burke built upon the work of Boethius, an early Christian philosopher of the sixth century, who made the seven circumstances of Cicero fundamental to the arts of prosecution and defense: who, what, where, by what means or with what, why, how, when (*quis, quid, ubi, quibus auxiliis, cur, quomodo, quando*). Burke combined *where* and *who* and called it "scene," and he conflated *how* and by *what means* and called it "agency" and established five circumstances as foundational for his grammar of motives.
Using as his key metaphor the dramatistic pentad, Burke maintained that all human action is meaningful and therefore persuasive, holding that motive exemplifies the basic forms of thought. He says,

"These forms of thought can be embodied profoundly or trivially, truthfully or falsely. They are equally present in systematically elaborated metaphysical structures, in legal judgments, in poetry and fiction, in political and scientific works, in news and in bits of gossip offered at random" (xv). Regardless of whether we agree or disagree with the purpose, with the character of a person, with how something was done, with the situation, or even if we want to call the act by other names, "be that as it may, any complete statement about motives will offer *some kind of* answers to these five questions: Act (what was done), Scene (when or where it was done), Agent (who did it), Agency (how was it done), Purpose (why was it done)" (xv). When we think Burke, we think motive.

Here's a thesis Burke might generate:

I love my dog, so I had it neutered.

Clearly driven by the motive of emotion, Burke would justify the act of neutering his dog.

Young, Becker, and Pike

Richard E. Young, Alton L. Becker, and Kenneth L. Pike in *Rhetoric: Discovery and Change* offer a heuristic procedure that identifies perspectives based on physics: particle, wave, field—and contrast, variation, and distribution. They believe any unit of experience could be viewed as static, dynamic, or as if in a network of relationships—as part of a larger network, or—to use their term—field.

As for persuasion in this schema, Young, Becker, and Pike state, "The purpose of the procedure is not to turn you into an intellectual machine that gathers information mechanically, but to guide and stimulate your intelligence, particularly your intuition, which is able to deal with enormous complexity in an original way" (128). When we think Young, Becker, and Pike, we think physics.

Here's a thesis hypothetically generated by Young, Becker, and Pike:

Examination of multiple breeds leads the dog owner to conclude: neutered dogs are healthy dogs.

Taken relationally, the particle "dog" is the one owned, the wave is the change from not neutered to neutered, and "multiple breeds" represent the field. The business of neutering would be considered not just as static *dog* but as field of dogs in relationship to other dogs.

Stephen Toulmin

Exchanging logical *theory* for logical *practice*, Stephen Toulmin eschews traditional terms as possibly prejudicial, so he provides a new model. Toulmin's *The Uses of Argument* includes the *claim*, which is based on *evidence* or *data*. He calls general statements that move the claim to the evidence or data *warrants*. *Backing* supports the warrants, *qualifiers* limit the claim, and *conditions of rebuttal* or *counterarguments* may be exceptions to the claim. When we think of Toulmin, we think about the discipline of jurisprudence, what Toulmin calls "the rational process."

Here's a typical Toulmin thesis:

Neutered dogs prevent unwanted litters.

Based on a clearly stated claim, which in turn is based on evidence (to be presented in the paper), Toulminites might limit the claim with the qualifier "unwanted." In this way, the argument is set up. Toulmin holds that "Logic is concerned with the soundness of the claims we make—with the solidity of the grounds we produce to support them, the firmness of the backing we provide for them" (7). In short, Toulmin considers logic and generalized jurisprudence as the procedures and categories by which claims can be argued and settled.

IV. PRESENT-DAY PERSUASION: A COMMENTARY

Recently in the *New York Times Magazine* (Oct. 3, 2010), we read "this is the rhetoric of crisis and desperation" (36). Although Mark Leibovich was not addressing persuasion, he made us think how "crisis and desperation" describe persuasion today. No longer concerned with truth or even eloquence, the rule of persuasion seems to be (pardon the oversimplifying and underconceptualizing) say whatever you want to say, say it again and again and again. Say it loudly and softly. Use all the media. Put it on Facebook. Tweet it on Twitter. Send it out in mass e-mails, on blogs. Make it a talking point. Say it repeatedly. Eventually enough people will believe it because of sheer repetition. It will begin to sound familiar and therefore it will begin to sound "true."

Today's boundaries, seemingly no longer Aristotelian or Quintilian, are marked best, perhaps, by personal or ideological agendas, moral codes or lack of them, and personal aggrandizement. Truths, facts, credibility, logic, evidence all seem quaint somehow. Testimony is suspect. One can tamper with statistics. The mantra now for the persuasive argument is repetition. For example, *Neutering makes for clean dogs, cleaner dogs, perhaps the cleanest dogs.* This thesis would then be repeated throughout a paper, over and over again *ad nauseam.*

If ever there were a time for students to study persuasion so as not to be sucked in by fast-talking radio hosts, TV personalities, overnight celebrities, or even unordained preachers, it is in today's global environment. Studying persuasion in order to write convincing papers in school and for tests is a noble purpose, but knowing the reasonableness of argument, recognizing the power of facts, and understanding the credentials of the person or persons persuading rises up as a necessary life skill.

MODEL

1. Brainstorm relevant issues.
2. Choose one, for example, the issue of school uniforms.
3. Think aloud the process of writing a thesis using the different rhetorical schools (but not necessarily all the schools) taken in this chapter. Caveat: In teaching persuasion, we are not suggesting students emulate the Sophists or vapid repetition to make their point. Rather, good writing teachers want their students to learn how to use sound logic to win their arguments or make their points.

We offer here a model orchestrated by a teacher and her class.

Teacher: If I were against mandating school uniforms, I'd have to decide which of the rhetorical stances would serve me best.

Plato would love the truth that they save money, but I don't want to go there. Anyway that wouldn't be good for me because I am not in favor of uniforms.

I don't want to be Sophist because I want my argument to be sound, not based on something spurious or manipulative. I could go with Aristotle's approach and just say, "Uniforms should not be mandated in public schools." I could find lots of evidence to support that plus if I took a survey of kids in my class, I am sure they would agree with me—especially the girls.

Burke appeals to me, too, but it seems too obvious to state the motive, so I don't think I'd find writing that as challenging, but being partial to science, I really like the physics stance. What fun to fool around with the particle, wave, field theory in relation to uniforms. I bet I'd be the only one to do that. And I could work that survey I intend to conduct into the distribution part of the theory.

I'm thinking that I could show the particle as ordinary kids content with the status quo and move to the kids who are into change, the ones who change for change sake. Then morph into the kids who don't change just to change but who want to be part of the group who follows the trends.

My conclusion will show the results of the survey (of course, I am hypothesizing that the kids I interview will not want uniforms). That way I can end with a real kicker.

So help me write my thesis, class. Let's call it a "working thesis statement (WTS)" because I might modify it as you give me suggestions.

At this point, various theses are written on the board or document camera. Each is discussed but finally the students decide on: "Mandated school uniforms go against what trendy students want to wear at school."

APPLICATION

Following the model above, students choose an issue and follow their thinking; they end with a working thesis statement they can place somewhere in the history of persuasion.

Since this is just practice in learning the different rhetorical schools of thought, students need not write a paper based on the thesis, just defend it in terms of its historical and rhetorical underpinnings. (See Appendix A, "A Suggested Mnemonic Device for Students to Remember the Major Rhetoricians or a Quick Guide for Debaters.")

CHAPTER 2

THE FOUR BASICS OF THE PERSUASIVE ESSAY

> A way of seeing is also a way of not seeing.
>
> —Kenneth Burke

Just as having a finger on the pulse of history helps students understand why they write what they write, having a finger—or several fingers—on the basics that make persuasive writing effective helps students achieve what they aim to say. We have distilled these basics into four manageable units to enhance learning: length, rhetorical stance, organization, and structure.

I. LENGTH

The first basic of persuasion is length. The digital age has changed everything. Once, we lingered long in persuasive papers, going into great depth, offering multi-arguments, even injecting figurative language. While the *New York Times* still publishes extended, more in-depth pieces, *Time*, *Newsweek*, and other popular magazines offer one-page essays, microstructured persuasions. No one seems to have the time or inclination for drawn-out discourse on an issue. So the length of a persuasive essay has become less a matter of scale and more a matter of strategy. Now we get in and get out, especially on tests.

Students who are made aware of the limitations and requirements for the persuasive essays they are writing do better than those students with one formula. What does the AP exam require? What about the SAT? What does this teacher or that professor expect? What about the state test? State-mandated tests vary—some are two pages, some longer; Texas has moved to a one-page essay. Other states have no page requirement in lieu of a time requirement.

Knowing what is expected and practicing that expectation help students write with confidence. We recommend teachers share with students the rubrics and examples from a variety of tests. We further recommend students practice writing to the highest point value of each rubric for each essay. There is no justification for sharing the lower-point rubrics because that invites the minimal. It's the maximum expectation all teachers and students should strive to achieve.

II. RHETORICAL STANCE

The second basic in persuasive writing—rhetorical stance—is pure Aristotle. Stance is all about adjusting tone and purpose to different audiences. Here the student chooses a stand on a given topic with a keen eye on the audience. The purpose is not to manipulate in the Sophist sense but to better garner arguments, evidence that will convince. Rhetorical stance also invites "being an insider" in order to get into the mind of that audience. What register of language would work best: instrumental, regulatory, contractual, perpetuating, personal? (See Appendix B, "Registers of Language Defined.")

Given the present-day abbreviation of the essay, writing it has become one of writing a thesis, making an assertion—a claim, to use Toulmin's term—and then proving it. Active reasoning insinuates the essence of persuasive writing. Writers of persuasive pieces take a stand on an issue and then explain the point (their thesis statement) and offer evidence in such a way that readers literally change their point of view.

A persuasive essay intends to cause the reader to do, think, or believe something different after reading it; it aims to change the reader.

Persuasion demands that the word arrangement, the syntax, conveys what matters to the writer so that the reader begins to care about that, too. More than any other writing, persuasion cements a partnership. Neeld calls persuasive writing "the most transformational mode" because its aim is not simply sharing or transferring information, perceptions, or opinions, but the writer makes "a commitment to have the reader think about something in a certain way" (278).

This suggests that the writer thoroughly know the topic *and* the audience in order to persuade from a knowledge vantage, using apt, clear, and lively prose. When taking a rhetorical stance, we recommend the following:

- convey immediately what the reader should do or believe;
- concentrate on the thesis, controlling idea, or central idea—the point of the persuasion;
- indicate knowledge of the topic; be an "insider";
- show the audience ways that appeal to its needs or wants;
- present the argument in an apt, clear, and lively prose;
- help the reader relate to the information through appropriate language and tone;
- engage the reader in one area of change;
- deliver what was promised in the thesis through a coherent, cohesive delivery system;
- make clear what the reader should do as a result of reading the essay.

Students need to recognize the fact that writing a persuasive essay on a topic is not about belief or dogma. Writing a persuasive essay is about *today* the writer wants to persuade this point. Think of it like friends—the friend you have today may be your "frienemy" tomorrow.

III. ORGANIZATION

Organization is the third basic to consider when writing a persuasive essay. In the second edition of *Acts of Teaching*, we state that "*Organization*, a slippery word in writing, slides in and around other words such as *focus* or *coherence*, *unity*, even *clarity*—all abstract terms to the neophyte student writer" (31). We go on to explain the author's purpose as foundational in making decisions about the organization of a paper. That concept bears repeating here, so we emphasize that in no other mode is the author's purpose more important than in persuasion.

Syllogistic Reasoning

While persuasion may adopt many modes—including the narrative—a parable with a lesson to convince, for example, the genre chosen most often is the essay. Sound persuasive essays build upon the logic of syllogistic reasoning. In *Prior Analytics*, Aristotle defines the syllogism as "a discourse in which, certain things having been supposed, something different from the things supposed results of necessity because these things are so" (24b18–20). Said more simply, a syllogism, composed of **two** statements (a major and minor premise), enables a conclusion (an inference) to be drawn from them.

The Syllogism

The word *syllogism* comes from the Greek (of course) and actually means conclusion or inference. For example:

> *All human beings are mortal. (major premise)*
> *Joan is a human being. (minor premise)*
> *Therefore, Joan is mortal. (conclusion)*

In the young adult sci-fi novel *Mistborn* by Brandon Sanderson, Eland and Jastes discuss aristocrats and skaa (the slave-like people controlled by the aristocrats). Eland uses syllogistic reasoning to persuade Jastes that Valette, a pretend noblewoman but really skaa, is a person just like they are.

> That's not the point, Jastes, she *fooled* us. If we can't tell the difference between a skaa and a noblewoman, [major premise] that means that the skaa can't be very different from us. [minor premise] And, if they're not that different from us, what right do we have treating them as we do?" [conclusion] (528)

Students don't easily come to the appropriate conclusion or inference when given syllogisms. Teachers need to provide much practice in this area.

Deduction and Induction

Over time the logic of the syllogism morphed into the logic of syllogistic thinking or as it is sometimes called—syllogistic reasoning. Syllogistic reasoning, based on the concept of the syllogism, offers arguments that are classified as deductive and inductive.

Deduction
Deduction begins with a general statement—*All human beings are mortal*—from which a specific conclusion is drawn—*Joan is mortal*. (See previous example.) Organizing an essay that begins with generalities and proceeds to specificities is called a deductively organized essay.

To secure deduction in students' minds, show them an inverted equilateral triangle—point down—as a graphic representation of deduction. Think of the prefix in *decreases* and *deduction* to help them distinguish it from induction. Remember: the word *deduct* means to subtract. Deductive reasoning begins with a broad statement and whittles away to a specific point (see Figure 2.1).

Induction
The reverse process is called induction. Induction begins with specific statements that lead to a generalization.

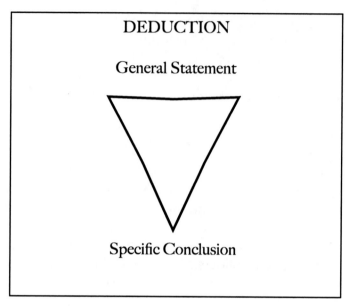

Figure 2.1

An inductive syllogism would read:

Peach A is green, feels hard, tastes sour.
Peach B is green, feels hard, tastes sour.
Peach C is green, feels hard, tastes sour.
Peach D is green, feels hard, tastes sour.
Therefore, peaches that are green and feel hard will
taste sour.

Some people call induction the scientific method because scientists work with vast amounts of data before reaching a conclusion. So organizing an essay that begins with specifics and proceeds to a generalization is called an inductively organized essay.

To secure induction in students' minds, show them an equilateral triangle—point up—as a graphic representation of induction. Think of the prefix in *increases* and *induction* to help them distinguish it from deduction. Inductive reasoning begins with a specific and then adds another and another on its way to a broad or general statement (see Figure 2.2).

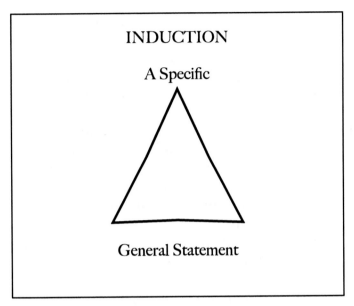

Figure 2.2

IV. STRUCTURE

The fourth basic of persuasive writing is its structure. All too often neophyte writers and teachers of writing confuse structure with formula. "Give me a structure! Kids need a structure!" they exclaim. The results, unfortunately, are often some artificially contrived formulae—so many paragraphs, so many sentences in each paragraph, and so on.

Joyce often tells the story of two gentlemen in her college freshman writing class who were arguing in a corner of the room. "May I help you?" she asked.

One wheeled around and said with great conviction, "My senior English teacher told me every paragraph had to be seven sentences and he says his senior English teacher told him every paragraph had to be five sentences." With great anticipation in their eyes they looked to her—after all this was college—here they would get the straight answer.

She wanted to shout, "Six!" Forevermore they would quote her, immortalize her. But, of course, she didn't. Rather she explained and showed the difference between a formulaic essay and an authentic one.

No matter how seductively easy it seems to expose students to a simple formula, it is academic fraud. Formula writing is dishonest, it doesn't make for good habits, it doesn't foster clear thinking, and it certainly destroys any logic. Giving students a formula is tantamount to giving students a 6″ by 6″ box and saying, "Fit your body into it."

> *Spider's Voice* by Gloria Skurzynski captures the horror of what happens when fitting a body (meaning) to a form (formula). This fascinating novel takes place in the twelfth century. Aran, a mute teenager, is sold to a dealer of human oddities who welds him into a metal vest to stunt his growth so he would grow into a "spider" with disproportionately long arms and legs. When we give students a formula, we are inviting written oddities.

Students produce unnatural deformities using formulae. Good writing calls upon the writer to find a focus, to develop an idea, and to think it through. Good writing is not fitting focus into a predetermined formula. Instead of formulae, give students patterns.

Four Patterns for the Persuasive Essay

The four patterns suggested here for the persuasive essay come from Kenneth A. Bruffee's *A Short Course in Writing*. We have worked with these since the mid-1970s and while permutations may be made, we find these four basic patterns serve students well. Bruffee himself states that these are not the only patterns, but they are good ones. He contends when students become facile in using these patterns, they develop confidence that eventually enables them to make up variations, explore other patterns, and even invent their own entirely new patterns (26).

The basic pattern is introduction, body, conclusion:

- An introduction primes the reader and clearly states the thesis, controlling idea, or central idea. (More about writing the thesis in Chapter 3.)

  Remember: Do not write the introduction first. Write the thesis first and then introduce it.

- The body of the essay may be one or multiple paragraphs given the complexity of the thesis, time, and page constraints. Here coherence and clarity rule.
- The conclusion, usually brief, ties the essay with a bow.

There is more in-depth instruction on what constitutes each pattern in Chapter 3 and how to put them together for a paper in Chapter 4. Here we are simply defining them.

Pattern 1: Equal Arguments
Choose this pattern if the evidence or support for the thesis is about the same quality. In some ways this is the easiest pattern to follow. Place each piece of evidence or support in a separate paragraph. For example, there may be compelling facts that would go into one paragraph and equally compelling statistics in another paragraph.

Pattern 2: Strawman
This pattern takes care of the problem of having evidence that rises up against the thesis, but the evidence can be refuted. Lawyers favor this sophisticated form. Give the thesis. Follow it with a paragraph or two that develops opposition to the thesis. Then follow the opposition with a paragraph or two that refutes the opposition and in that way proves the thesis. (The term "strawman" comes from the straw men placed on wooden horses during the Middle Ages to be used in jousting practice by the knights. Apparently the knight and nobility first forced peasants to be their targets, but just as apparently over time this must have led to a shortage of peasants! Hence the notion of placing a man made out of straw on a wooden "horse." The idea was to knock down these straw men.) So, too, with this pattern: The idea is to logically "knock down" the opposing argument.

Subpattern 2. Strawman Plus
This subpattern combines strawman with equal arguments. Bruffee calls it "Strawman and One Argument in Defense" (84). We call it "Strawman Plus" because often there are more arguments in defense that may be made.

Strawman Plus presents the opposing argument and its refutation but then goes on to present the reasons or evidence that support the thesis. Hence the word *plus* as it may be one piece of supporting evidence or several.

Pattern 3: Concession

Concession, like strawman, acknowledges existing evidence that goes against the thesis, but this evidence cannot be refuted. To ignore it would be the major fallacy called "half-truth" (see Appendix D). So the writer acknowledges it but then offers stronger proof in favor of the thesis. Politicians adore concession because instead of refuting the thesis, they concede to its validity only to then offer a stronger defense. With concession, the operative word is *but*.

Pattern 4: Nestorian Order

Whether this pattern is named after the monk Nestorius, known for his eloquent preaching, or after the monk Nestor, The Chronicler, known for piecing together the fragments of church chronicles, remains in dispute. Nevertheless, this form allows arguments to be presented to their psychologically powerful advantage. Students choose this pattern if there is an abundance of not equally weighted but significant evidence or if they don't know all the evidence equally. This pattern, favored by preachers, states the thesis, then organizes the arguments by presenting the second best argument first, followed by minor arguments. It ends with the best, strongest argument. So strong is this pattern that one student asked us, "Is this cheating?" We explained that it is not cheating to show your knowledge in the best possible way.

MODEL

Return students to the theses they wrote for the application at the end of Chapter 1. Based on those theses, discuss what pattern would best serve each thesis. For example: The thesis example in Chapter 1 states "Mandated school uniforms goes against what trendy students want to wear at school," which suggests digging into what trendy students might want to wear. Invite students to think which of the four patterns would best fit that essay. As students suggest patterns, invite an explanation of the thinking behind each suggestion.

Nota bene: For testing situations, we recommend Equal Arguments and Nestorian Order. These patterns enable students to present their arguments clearly and concisely. The danger with the other two patterns in testing situations rests with readers who may miss the sophistication of setting up an argument only to refute it or validate it and then present their argument or arguments in defense of the thesis. Also, time and space become serious considerations.

This both refines thinking and reviews the patterns and characteristics of a good thesis.

Students might suggest that they would start with one ordinary kid who follows the status quo, and then move to the kids who are into change. They might choose Nestorian Order already intending to end with the survey—the kicker—the strongest argument. The important piece in this part of the process is the explanation.

APPLICATION

Students then take the remaining theses and follow the model. They share which of the patterns of persuasion they would choose and orally justify their choices. (They may do this as a class or in small groups.)

Again, they do not yet write this out; this is an oral thinking exercise. But again be sure to discuss the syllogistic reasoning that will be needed for each pattern of choice.

CHAPTER 3

FOUR GUIDES FOR WRITING PERSUASIVELY

> The process of working through an argument is the process of inquiry.
>
> —George Hillocks, Jr.

G uides are not mandates. In fact, one definition of a guide is "a model." This chapter provides four quick guides or models to keep in mind when approaching the persuasive essay: finding the topic, crafting the thesis, defending it, and ending it. This embraces process and ensures an end product.

GUIDE ONE: FIND THE TOPIC

As Janet Emig tells us, "Writing is a mode of learning," so when we write something persuasive—perhaps more than in any other genre—we need to know our topic and know it well. We need to become an insider. We need to research and collect data on our topic. And in the persuading we also learn. Hillocks says it this way, "Good argument begins with looking at the data that are likely to become the evidence" (26). Without fodder, the raw material—the data—from which to draw evidence, we weakly persuade.

So the work begins. Inquiry is all about digging into an issue or discovering some salient point and then taking a rhetorical stand on that issue or point. Good lawyers live for that one piece of data that clinches the argument, is indisputable, or that totally knocks down any counterarguments. But not all data are clear-cut, so we look for data that scaffolds the support, explains, or demonstrates the truth of our topic, or we look for data that seriously jeopardize the opposing argument. Inquiry at this stage in the process is crucial.

Using the Carroll/Wilson Inquiry Schemata answers Hillocks's call for "analysis of any data (verbal and nonverbal texts, materials, surveys and samples)" (26). Notice in Figure 3.1 the process begins with a blending of previous knowledge, experiences, and observations that yield a topic. Then students

- take notes on that topic
- raise questions
- make predictions
- create a hypothesis (a working thesis statement [WTS]).

Deeper insights evolve around prewriting as the reading, researching, thinking, evaluating, and talking take place. All this contributes recursively to the topic.

Afterward, then and only then, students construct a thesis statement. Without this preliminary study, writing a thesis statement becomes ephemeral, somewhat like trying to grab the wind. With the proper priming, however, students construct a viable working thesis statement and proceed to write their conclusions, connect that thesis to previous knowledge and experiences, and organize the data—again feeling comfortable about reaching back while moving

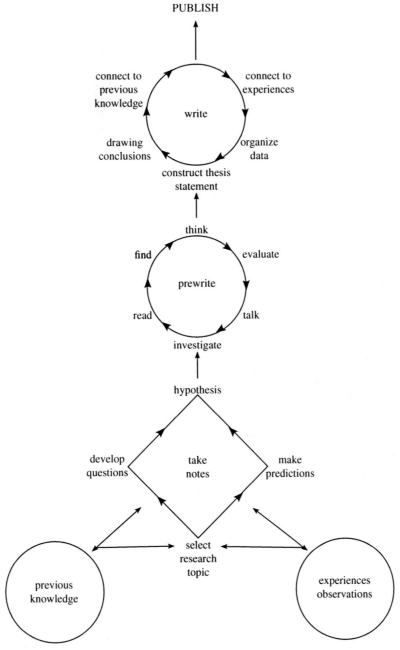

Figure 3.1. The Carroll/Wilson Inquiry Schemata

forward. Sometimes in research, especially at this point in the process, students discover they need to read more, think more, and evaluate more deeply, hence the often-repeated recursive back and forward movement of the process. This willingness to dig ever deeper, to re-evaluate the data, marks the good researcher. Students cannot craft a truly persuasive paper, a sound argument, without going through this process.

Testing Situations

In testing situations when the topic—sometimes even the thesis—is given, students familiar with the Carroll/Wilson Inquiry Schemata tap its subschemes—the schemes within the schemata. After using the schemata for persuasive assignments in class, students have a firm handle on the process. Then in a testing situation, they easily call upon those subschemes: previous knowledge, experiences, and observations. They know the value of jotting notes as a means of giving substance to their thinking about the topic; and they develop questions and make predictions.

It would be natural, then, for students to do a bit of prewriting. (They eagerly seize this opportunity, unlike some students who wonder why those extra pages are even in the test booklet.) Unable to talk during the test, they have the schemata in their heads to evaluate what they have prewritten. When they do write, they have organizational patterns (see Chapter 4) from which to choose, so they make logical connections and draw logical conclusions.

Juxtapose this with the student without strategies—with perhaps only a formula—who goes into such testing situations much like an unarmed person going into battle.

GUIDE TWO: CRAFT THE THESIS STATEMENT

Because the thesis statement is the writer's promise to the reader, it belongs early in the paper, somewhere in its introduction. Without a clear thesis early on, the reader wanders around the words searching for the idea or simply gives up the reading out of confusion. It's not unlike driving to an unknown destination without a map—the driver would get lost, never get there, never get back on course, or would waste time driving about. With a map—a thesis—the road is clear and sure.

To craft a sound thesis, students need exposure to the characteristics of a good thesis statement. Over the years, we have suggested these simple ABCs and DOs and DON'Ts.

The **ABCs** for writing a good thesis:

> It must be an Assertion.
> The writer must **B**e an insider.
> It must be Clearly written.

The **DOs and DON'Ts** of a good thesis:

Dos

- Express the point of the paper.

  Ex: Tourists find Mexico City best in springtime.

- Make it defensible.

  Ex: Travel changes people's perspectives about their place in the world.

- Be specific.

  Ex: The United States should pull out of Afghanistan.

- Be concise.

  Ex: Microwaves hasten cooking time.

- Use strong verbs if possible.

  Ex: Exposure to chemicals harms children.

- Write a statement—a declarative sentence.

  Ex: Good government tells its people the truth.

Don'ts

- DON'T bifurcate.

  Ex: Brains function for thinking and eating.

- DON'T describe the strategy of the paper.

  Ex: I am going to persuade you to read *Water for Elephants*.

- DON'T be wordy.

  Ex: River Gull inflatable kayaks make adventure serendipitous because you can carry one in your car, blow it up anywhere, and paddle it anytime you come upon a scenic lake or river.

- DON'T write the thesis as a question.

  Ex: Do you believe in the death penalty?

REMEMBER: A muddled thesis makes a muddled paper.

Bruffee validates the importance of the thesis statement—what we call *the importance of the pith*—saying, "Suppose a writer was told, 'Save only one sentence—the sentence that says exactly what the paper says. Throw the rest away'" (43). That sentence would be the thesis sentence—the pith—the essence. Knowing that singular fact gives the writer power.

The word *thesis* itself gives us a clue to its importance. Coming from the Latin and Greek, it means *the act of placing* or *laying down*; it means *to position, to propose,* or *to claim.* In fact, the thesis statement focuses the entire paper; it controls it. Without it, the paper is dangerously close to being nothing more than a jumble of thoughts.

Over time and across grade levels and subjects, the thesis statement has been and continues to be called many things. When reading, we ask students to find the *main idea, central idea,* or *theme,* whereas in writing, we caution students to have a *focus, controlling idea, central idea, thesis statement, assertion, claim,* or *proposition.*

Think of the thesis as the main event around which everything revolves. It's like the vows at a wedding. The flowers, attire, decorations, cake, rings, gifts, music, and food, while contributing to the event, are not the vows. Vows solidify the point and promise—the pith; everything else supports them.

GUIDE THREE: DEFEND IT

Stephen E. Toulmin, in his chapter "The Layout of Arguments" in *The Uses of Argument,* talks about how the *claim* must be based on evidence, how the *warrant* explains that claim, and how *backing* supports the warrants. It's commonsensical, really, if you claim something, you should be able to provide evidence to back that claim. That's the stuff of persuasion. The defense in an essay, like the defense lawyer in the courtroom, argues for the thesis or persuades in favor of the thesis in a coherent, organized way, using organic transitions. In other words: The thesis must be defended.

How do you back up a thesis or a claim? In keeping with the title of this book, we suggest four major ways:

1. Facts and statistics
2. Expert testimony
3. Examples
4. Anecdotes

Facts and Statistics

A fact is something that may be objectively verified, something real or actual. That we are writing this book is an incontrovertible fact. Facts are powerful persuaders because they are difficult to dispute.

Statistics, facts on steroids, usually give information in exact or estimated numbers. Saying "After tallying enrollment sheets, we know *there are 2,105 students in X High School*" is one way to present a statistic, or saying "*Our survey shows that three out of every four kids wear flip flops in the summer*" is another way. Tables, graphs, maps, columns, codes, timelines, diagrams, different fonts, and other means of visualization (now extended because of the computer) enhance the use of statistics, making them easier to see and comprehend.

Expert Testimony

Expertise exists on a rolling scale. Thanks in part to *Wikipedia*, where anyone can edit unprotected pages and submit edits for protected ones, no longer is an expert is an expert is an expert—to take great liberties with Gertrude Stein. With information billowing out at the rate of 2.5 billion documents with a rate of growth of 7.3 million pages per day just on the World Wide Web, with deep Web claiming to be 400 to 550 times larger, first checking the credentials of the "expert" is a must. Also, if many different and credible researchers in a given field say the same or similar things, then the evidence they provide holds greater weight. (See Testimonial in Appendix D.)

Examples

Examples lend specificity to any argument. In the second edition of *Acts of Teaching* we define an example (along with illustration and instance) as "a specific thing, person, or event that illuminates a general thing, person, or event" (140).

We may claim that e-books are quickly replacing paper books. We may find a statistic such as NOOKBooks alone publishes more than one million titles. But we may pull those generalizations into a more specific reality through an example of a teacher who attended one of our recent presentations. Whenever we referenced a book, she simply ordered it as an e-book. At the conclusion of the session, she showed us her "page" with all the books we had mentioned already downloaded and ready to read.

By giving that example, we bring the wonders down to the personal level, one that most often clinches the argument.

Anecdotes

An anecdote is simply a story—a brief narrative. Anecdotes have always been our favorite way to persuade. When trying to convince teachers, for example, of some new strategy, we often persuade them by telling a story about the strategy, its use, how the kids responded to it, or how the teacher modified or tweaked it. Everything is there—characters, setting, action, the tension of trying something new, and the resolution. And because humans are hardwired for stories, it takes. Sometimes, though, we end our presentation with an anecdote that reinforces the strategy in a poignant or humorous way.

Of course, all this evidence has to be woven into the fabric of the essay in a logical, maybe even syllogistic, way. It must be organized. And that will be taken up in great detail in Chapter 4.

GUIDE FOUR: END IT

When the purpose of the essay is to persuade, some consideration should be given to its conclusion. Some tests or assignments will require one- or two-sentence endings because of time or page limit; other essays will allow for a lengthier conclusion. For the persuasive essay, we suggest four possibilities: the summary, the call to action, the clincher, or a contemplative ending.

The Summary

Perhaps due to the third piece of advice in the admonition, "tell what you are going to tell, tell it, and then tell what you told," summary is the most *used* and *abused* of conclusions. That third piece of advice suggests a retelling that results in boring or redundant summaries. Forget it. Rather opt for a unique summary, one that adds a fresh thought or a new dimension to the text. That makes a persuasive paper powerful to the last period.

We have several examples in this category, but our favorite comes from Kenneth P. Czech's *Snapshot: America Discovers the Camera*. After pages of words and photographs about the history of the camera in America, this book richly concludes:

> As *Life* publisher Henry Luce noted in 1936, photographs allowed people
> To see life—to see the world, to eyewitness great events; to watch the faces of the poor and the gestures of the proud

... to see strange things ... to see man's work ... to see and be amazed; to see and be instructed.

Most of all, photographs allowed Americans to see themselves.

Now that's a summary.

The Call to Action

This conclusion perfectly fits the purpose of persuasion because after the argument and the evidence, it challenges the reader to do something about it.

In her book *Toxic People*, Lillian Glass persuades people to avoid those who make their lives miserable. She concludes with a call to action that rings like a battle cry:

There will always be people in the world that we may find toxic, but we have options available that equip us to overcome their toxic influence. We need to stop the hatred and prejudice and jealousy and victimization and start pulling together as a people, as a nation and as a world!

Don't you just want to stand up and cheer?

The Clincher

In *Conclusions: The Unicorns of Composition*, I say this about the clincher: "Sometimes, when all is said and done, a succinct fact, statement, or remark skewers the piece best. The craft of condensing any genre into one or two ending statements, facts, or remarks speaks to the skill of the author" (113).

To us the clincher of all clinchers comes from Ted Sorensen's *Kennedy*:

The next morning, in Fort Worth, he [Kennedy] expressed confidence that "because we are stronger ... our chances for security, our chances for peace, are better than they have been in the past." That afternoon in Dallas, he was shot dead.

The word *dead* hits the reader like the shot itself—Kennedy wasn't just shot; he was shot dead. That raw fact hits the reader like the bullet itself and clinches the argument.

Contemplative Ending

Persuasive writing invites cognitive chewing. We once had a professor who always cut off debate *before* everything was thoroughly discussed. "That way," he said, "you continue to think, consider, and reflect on what was said." So, too, with a persuasive paper—the contemplative ending leaves the reader thinking. This ending gives the reader something to mull over or ruminate upon at the end.

Natalie Babbitt hangs readers forever on a pensive hook with the last sentence in *Tuck Everlasting* when Tuck says of the toad in the road, "Durn fool thing must think it's going to live forever." We think Babbitt's ending would make a fine contemplative ending to any persuasive essay on the topic of the infinite—not to mention the significance of allusion.

When students learn to deliver a good piece of persuasive text, they will be on their way to becoming masters of persuasion or CEOs of advertising companies!

MODEL

Choose a thesis from Appendix C to use as a model. Go thorough the process—aloud—deciding if it's a good thesis, one that meets the characteristics of a good thesis, or not. If it doesn't meet the criteria (and it is best for modeling purposes to choose one that doesn't), work with the students on crafting it into a thesis that meets the criteria.

APPLICATION

- Distribute the theses in Appendix C to students, choosing appropriate ones for the grade level.

- Divide the theses into groups according to the number of students—anywhere from three to five theses for each group of students.
- Divide students into groups.
- Each group decides if each thesis they received qualifies or does not qualify as a good thesis based on its characteristics.

When sharing: If the thesis is a good one, the group points out why. If the thesis does not meet the criteria, the group revises it by rewriting it in a better way. Each group shares and gives their explanation.

CHAPTER 4

FOUR PATTERNS FOR TEACHING THE PERSUASIVE ESSAY

Knowledge is a social construct, a consensus among the members of a community of knowledgeable peers.

—Kenneth A. Bruffee

Building on Bruffee's four patterns, which he calls "a new model for learning the principles of discursive writing" (1), we, too, want students to experience the mental processes essential to writing persuasively. Rather than just telling students how to organize and write a persuasive essay, we believe in taking the students through the process. Bear in mind these four patterns are forms, not formulae. We think of them as patterns orchestrated to help students move up the Carroll/Wilson Inquiry Schemata (see Figure 3.1) by

- discovering or uncovering ideas
- writing a clear thesis statement
- defending their ideas
- understanding how to show relationships through coherence.

FOURTEEN-DAY IMPLEMENTATION MODEL

DAY ONE

- Divide the class into groups of about four or five students.

- Provide large sheets of butcher paper and colored markers for each group.

- Explain the read-aloud strategy to give students a purpose for listening. Tell students that in this case as the teacher (or designated student) reads, they are to listen carefully for possible issues that would make good working theses statements (WTS) and jot them down.

- Ask students to think of issues that pop into their brains during the read-aloud.

- Read aloud a provocative piece of literature—this could be a short story, a piece of flash fiction, an essay from a recent newspaper or magazine, or a children's book such as *William's Doll* by Charlotte Zolotow, which suggests among other issues "boy toys" and "girl toys," or *Earrings!* by Judith Viorst, which brings up the topic—among others—of age and proper attire. *Ruby's Wish* by Shirin Yim Bridges generates discussion on educating women; *Owen* by Kevin Henkes and Cynthia Rylant's *The Ticky-Tacky Doll* foster thought on whether kids should bring toys from home to school as well as other concerns.

- After the read-aloud, students brainstorm issues suggested by the text.

- Display lists and discuss.

Nicole Frazier, Abydos trainer from Fort Bend Independent School District, offers the following suggestions:

Mélanie Watt's persuasive text, *Have I Got a Book for You!*, debunks all notions that persuasion equals boring essay. Mr. Al Foxword uses an array of persuasive tactics to convince readers they *must* buy his book. Using personal testimonies, compliments, statistics, incentives, and humor, *Have I Got a Book for You!* introduces persuasive strategies to students in a delightful way. After brainstorming the strategies Mr. Al uses to convince his audience, students dip their toes in the water and write a persuasive advertisement following Watt's guide—"Have I Got a ____ for You!"

In Mo Willems's *Don't Let the Pigeon Drive the Bus*, the bus driver leaves his bus under *your*—the reader's—control. While the pigeon desperately tries to convince *you* to let him drive the bus, all *you* can do is find clever and unique ways of saying NO. After reading the story straight through, I read it again, allowing time for writers to craft their responses to the pigeon's requests. Students then form groups of three and each take turns reading from the point of view of the bus driver, the pigeon, and the reader/writer. Students delight in listening and sharing. Again and again, they notice the pigeon's poor use of persuasion tactics, and they learn what *not* to do in their writing

The Great Kapok Tree by Lynne Cherry takes on a more serious tone and issue—our world's rainforests. Although a fictional story told from the point of view of creatures inhabiting a great kapok tree, Cherry includes maps, diagrams, and facts about the changing status of the world's rainforest. I use this text to introduce my students to the persuasive terms rhetorical stance, point of view, and central idea. As we read, we discuss the author's stance on the issue and consider the two opposing viewpoints (the animals versus the man with the ax). I then ask students to step out of the text and consider their own points of view. As students share, I ask them to reflect on how the author's central idea and message affected their own.

Frazier also suggests *Earrings!* by Judith Viorst, *Click, Clack, Moo: Cows That Type* by Doreen Cronin, *I Wanna Iguana* by Karen Kaufman Orloff, *Lincoln Tells a Joke: How Laughter Saved the President (and the Country)* by Kathleen Krull and Paul Brewer, and *Martin's Big Words: The Life of Dr. Martin Luther King, Jr.* by Doreen Rappaport.

DAY TWO

- Together prioritize the issues in order of interest.

- Students star those issues/topics that hold the highest interest for them.

- Then, using the criteria for writing a thesis statement, the teacher chooses a starred issue/topic and models writing it into a "working" thesis statement.

- Students take the remaining starred issues/topics for practice. Using sentence strips, they write these issues/topics into "working" theses statements.

- Display. Discuss each statement according to the criteria.

- At this point, students read through all the choices and make a commitment to one. This becomes their "working thesis statement" (WTS).

DAY THREE

- Students spend this day investigating the WTS of their choice, taking notes, developing questions, making predictions, and then honing their "working" thesis.

- Discuss the process. Share.

DAY FOUR

- Students find opposing views or contradictions to their thesis statements. The goal is to find at least one opposing view.

- Share.

DAY FIVE

- Give students six 5.5″ by 8.5″ index cards or six half sheets of regular notebook paper. Color is key. We suggest two yellow, two blue, and two green, but any three different colors work.

- Students label the yellow cards "PRO," the blue cards "CON," and the green cards "WTS" (for "pro and con theses statements").

- Allow time for students to write their WTS on the green cards.

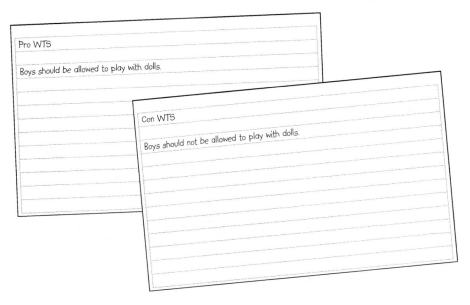

Pro WTS

Boys should be allowed to play with dolls.

Con WTS

Boys should not be allowed to play with dolls.

DAY SIX

- Students follow the Carroll/Wilson Inquiry Schemata by continuing to read, talk, evaluate, and research as they search for textual evidence and data for their prewriting.

- They evaluate their thesis statement in light of this continued research and revise it further.

DAY SEVEN

- Students evaluate their data, choosing one argument to write on each of the PRO cards. Teachers model this procedure by writing their own cards with PRO arguments and by providing extra cards for those who need them.

We chose Josh's cards as examples. His PRO cards read:

Pro Card One:

Argument in defense:

When boys play with dolls they learn how to nurture babies, a skill a boy will need when he has his own children.

Pro Card Two:

Quotations from book:

In the book it says "William wanted a doll...just as though he were its father and it were his child" (5 & 10).
"William's grandmother smiled. 'He needs it,' she said, 'to hug and to cradle and to take to the park so that when he's a father like you, he'll know how to take care of his baby and feed him and love him and bring him the things he wants, like a doll so that he can practice being a father" (30-32). The grandmother supports William's request by using the circle of life and the power of modeling to make a convincing argument in favor of William getting a doll. This supports my WTS because she is describing nurturing.

Pro Card Three:

Statistic I:

In these days when men and women share the responsibility of raising children, developing this sensitivity in boys early on is important. It readies their brains. Plus more men are taking care of their kids these days. According to Nijole V. Benokraitis in <u>Marriages & Families: Changes, Choices and Contraints</u>, "Of the 187 participants at FORTUNE MAGAZINE'S MOST POWERFUL WOMEN IN BUSINESS SUMMIT, 1/3 of the women's husbands were stay-at-home dads."

Pro Card Four:

Anecdote:

I talked to my father. He said because he had three sisters, two older and one younger, he was surrounded by dolls. But there weren't any boys in his neighborhood, so he played with his sisters. "We had fun making up characters," he said. "I remember once we played <u>The Wizard of Oz</u>. My oldest sister picked Dorothy. The other older sister chose Glenda, the Good Witch. They let me play, so I pretended my doll was the Wicked Witch of the West. My kid sister got to play Toto." Then my father said, "Son, I don't think dolls are good or bad playthings. I think it matters what you do with them."

Pro Card Five:

Fact:

Boys play with action figures such as G. I. Joes, Spider-Man, various sports figures, and figures from TV and movies such as <u>Star Wars.</u> Although they are called "figures," they are really dolls. So what's the difference?

Pro Card Six:

Statistic II:

British researchers Glenn Wilson and Qazi Rahman, authors of <u>Born Gay: The Psychobiology of Sex Orientation</u>, conclude after years of sifting through data, "Sexual orientation is something we are born with and not 'acquired' from our social environment."

1. *Argument in defense:* When boys play with dolls they learn how to nurture babies, a skill a boy will need when he has his own children.
2. *Quotations from book:* In the book it says "William wanted a doll . . . just as though he were its father and it were his child" (5 and 10). "William's grandmother smiled. 'He needs it,' she said, 'to hug and to cradle and to take to the park so that when he's a father like you, he'll know how to take care of his baby and feed him and love him and bring him the things he wants, like a doll so that he can practice being a father'" (30–32). The grandmother supports William's request by using the circle of life and the power of modeling to make a convincing argument in favor of William getting a doll. This supports my WTS because she is describing nurturing.
3. *Statistic I:* In these days when men and women share the responsibility of raising children, developing this sensitivity in boys early on is important. It readies their brains. Plus more men are taking care of their kids these days. According to Nijole V. Benokraitis in *Marriages & Families: Changes, Choices and Constraints*, "Of the 187 participants at *Fortune*

Magazine's Most Powerful Women in the Business Summit,
1/3 of the women's husbands were stay-at-home dads."

4. *Anecdote:* I talked to my father. He said because he had three
sisters, two older and one younger, he was surrounded by
dolls. But there weren't any boys in his neighborhood, so he
played with his sisters. "We had fun making up characters,"
he said. "I remember once we played *The Wizard of Oz.* My
oldest sister picked Dorothy. The other older sister chose
Glenda, the Good Witch. They let me play, so I pretended
my doll was the Wicked Witch of the West. My kid sister got
to play Toto." Then my father said, "Son, I don't think dolls
are good or bad playthings; I think it matters what you do
with them."

5. *Fact:* Boys play with action figures such as G.I. Joe, Spider-
Man, various sports figures, and figures from TV and movies
such as *Star Wars.* Although they are called "figures," they
are really dolls. So what's the difference?

6. *Statistic II:* British researchers Glenn Wilson and Qazi Rahman, authors of *Born Gay: The Psychobiology of Sex Orientation,* conclude after years of sifting through data, "Sexual
orientation is something we are born with and not 'acquired'
from our social environment."

- Students follow the same procedure for the CON cards. They write
one opposing argument on each of their CON cards. Teachers
model this procedure by writing their own cards with CON arguments and by providing extra cards for those who need them.
Josh's CON cards read:

> Con Card One:
>
> Argument against:
>
> Playing with dolls makes boys into sissies.

Con Card Two:

Quotations from book:

"Sissy, sissy, sissy!" said the boy next door. (11)
"Creepy" said his brother. "Sissy sissy" chanted the boy next door." (12)

Con Card Three:

Expert testimony:

"This kind of behavior can only lead to heartbreak and loneliness. It must be nipped in the bud or the children will become perverted, " says Monique Steinhome, child psychologist.

Con Card Four:

Example from the book:

To keep William from becoming a sissy, his father, uncomfortable with William's request, tries giving William toys the father considers more gender-appropriate such as a basketball and a train set.

Con Card Five:

Fact:

Boys playing with dolls goes against the norms of society. Good parents want their kids to be normal, so good parents discourage their kids from doing things that aren't normal, whether it's boys playing with dolls or girls playing with backhoes, or either playing with loaded guns. It goes against societal norms.

1. *Argument against:* Playing with dolls makes boys into sissies.
2. *Quotations from book:* "'Sissy, sissy, sissy!' said the boy next door. 'Creepy' said his brother. 'Sissy sissy' chanted the boy next door" (11 and 12).
3. *Expert testimony:* "This kind of behavior can only lead to heartbreak and loneliness. It must be nipped in the bud or the children will become perverted," says Monique Steinhome, child psychologist.
4. *Example from the book:* To keep William from becoming a sissy, his father, uncomfortable with William's request, tries giving William toys the father considers more gender appropriate such as a basketball and a train set.
5. *Fact:* Boys playing with dolls goes against the norms of society. Good parents want their kids to be normal, so good parents discourage their kids from doing things that aren't normal, whether it's boys playing with dolls or girls playing with backhoes, or either playing with loaded guns. It goes against societal norms.

DAY EIGHT

This is a crucial day when the writing must be modeled perhaps several times over several days.

- Either on another card or on paper that may be attached to the original, students begin the process of expounding, explaining, and elaborating upon the data on the card.

- Teachers model writing the four ways to defend a thesis (see Chapter 3). They show the difference between facts and statistics, and they show how to reference the sources. They give examples of expert testimony, and anecdotes that support the claim. Further they model how to integrate and embed these data into the composition. They also model the possibility of having an unused card or cards.

- Students work to integrate their data into the information so that it reads smoothly and makes its point.

We have always taught students not only how to find support for their theses but also how to integrate, punctuate, and reference that support. They follow five easy steps:

1. *Introduce the quotation.* A brief introduction places the quoted information in the context of the paper. The quotation should go with the flow of the text and not strike the reader as something inserted, perhaps as a requirement.

2. *Give the quotation.* Here attention must be given to accuracy. This is not an exercise in inferring. Misreading or misquoting changes the dynamic of the argument. The quotation must be copied exactly.

3. *Explain the quotation.* The quotation must be elaborated upon to ensure the reader understands its significance. Assuming the reader will see the connection between the quotation and text demands too much from the reader or could cause confusion.

4. *Punctuate the quotation correctly.* A direct quotation begins with an opening quotation mark and ends with a closing quotation mark. If any information must be inserted to make the sentence read properly, place it in brackets [ ]. Bracketed information indicates that it was not part of the original quotation.

5. *Cite the reference.* Check the reference style you are using: MLA, APA, Chicago MS, Turabian, Harvard, CGOS, CBE. Follow the same reference style throughout the paper. The key is consistency; do not change reference styles.

DAYS NINE through TWELVE

Using the cards as manipulatives, first the teacher arranges and rearranges his or her cards, using the think-aloud strategy so students have a model of the thinking process involved. Then each student arranges and rearranges his or her cards, experimenting with Bruffee's four organizational patterns.

> **Remember: The purpose is to help students see how the pattern enhances the argument—not how the argument is created by the pattern.**

After hearing *William's Doll*, Josh chose this as his WTS: *Boys should be allowed to play with dolls.*

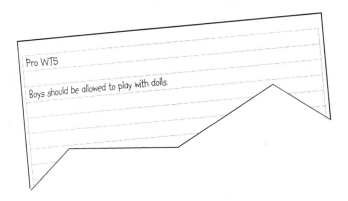

We chose Josh's cards as examples of how this four-patterned method works. Although some of his cards require further elaboration and research, for example, the reference to children's brains in PRO #3, Josh is ready to make some decisions. At this point in the process students actually experience the four patterns. The teacher models and explains each pattern, allowing the students time to study their cards, arranging and rearranging them accordingly.

Pattern **1**: Equal Arguments

Beginning with Equal Arguments, the teacher explains and models with his or her cards. While the easiest, this pattern works best when each argument has approximately equal strength. Using his PRO cards, Josh decided to go with what he considered three equal arguments. He placed them in the order as shown:

Pro WTS

Boys should be allowed to play with dolls.

Pro Card One:

Argument in defense:

When boys play with dolls they learn how to nurture babies, a skill a boy will need when he has his own children.

Pro Card Three:

Statistic 1:

In these days when men and women share the responsibility of raising children, developing this sensitivity in boys early on is important. It readies their brains. Plus more men are taking care of their kids these days. According to Nijole V. Benokraitis in Marriages & Families: Changes, Choices and Contraints, "Of the 187 participants at FORTUNE MAGAZINE's MOST POWERFUL WOMEN IN BUSINESS SUMMIT, 1/3 of the women's husbands were stay-at-home dads."

Pro Card Two:

Quotations from book:

In the book it says "William wanted a doll...just as though he were its father and it were his child" (5 & 10).
"William's grandmother smiled. 'He needs it,' she said, 'to hug and to cradle and to take to the park so that when he's a father like you, he'll know how to take care of his baby and feed him and love him and bring him the things he wants, like a doll so that he can practice being a father" (30-32). The grandmother supports William's request by using the circle of life and the power of modeling to make a convincing argument in favor of William getting a doll. This supports my WTS because she is describing nurturing.

Josh said, "I'm saving the anecdote from my father for my conclusion. I think the first three are about equal and follow coherently from argument to statistic to quotation. I think Dad's anecdote will clinch the paper. It will be one of those clincher conclusions."

Pattern **2**: Strawman

To use this pattern the data present an opposing argument or counterargument that cannot be ignored, but the data also present some information with which to refute it, or, continuing the metaphor of the "strawman" of the jousts, knock it down. For strawman, students consider their cards, evaluating them in light of finding one with data able to knock down an opposing argument. The teacher points out that arguments are rarely one-sided. If there is compelling opposition, it cannot be ignored, but the evidence in favor of the WTS should be strong enough to weaken or even destroy the opposing argument. Here's Josh's thinking:

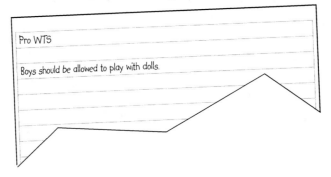

Pro WTS

Boys should be allowed to play with dolls.

    Josh presented #1 of his CON cards as his opposing argument because he thought he could knock down that argument by using fact #5 from his PRO cards. Here is how he laid out his strawman pattern:

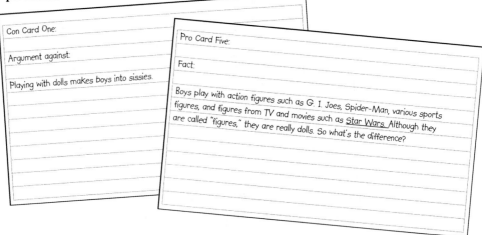

Con Card One:

Argument against:

Playing with dolls makes boys into sissies.

Pro Card Five:

Fact:

Boys play with action figures such as G. I. Joes, Spider-Man, various sports figures, and figures from TV and movies such as <u>Star Wars.</u> Although they are called "figures," they are really dolls. So what's the difference?

Josh arranged the cards but realized he would have to do much more work developing both the opposing argument and the refutation of that opposition, which give credence to the recursiveness of the process. So going through this process benefited him and others who think simply saying something is enough of an argument.

Subpattern 2: Strawman Plus

Here the teacher explained that the "plus" means that while the pattern is still strawman, the writer finds still another reason worth developing to defend the WTS. Josh simply added a new PRO to his existing cards. Here is how Josh shuffled his cards to accommodate strawman plus:

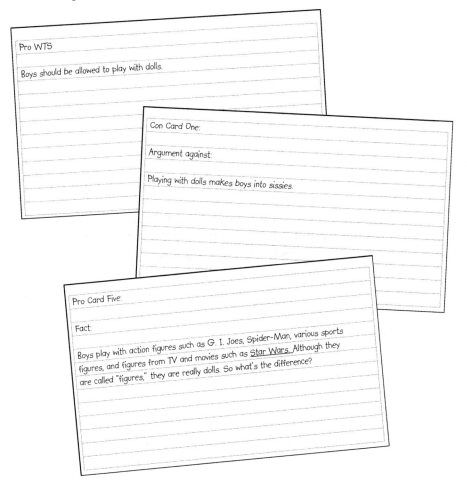

Pro WTS

Boys should be allowed to play with dolls.

Con Card One:

Argument against:

Playing with dolls makes boys into sissies.

Pro Card Five:

Fact:

Boys play with action figures such as G. I. Joes, Spider-Man, various sports figures, and figures from TV and movies such as Star Wars. Although they are called "figures," they are really dolls. So what's the difference?

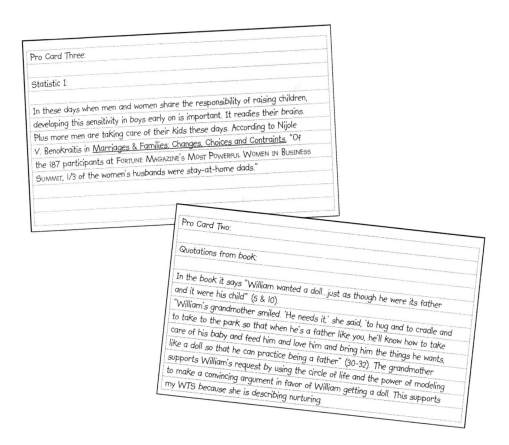

Pro Card Three:

Statistic I:

In these days when men and women share the responsibility of raising children, developing this sensitivity in boys early on is important. It readies their brains. Plus more men are taking care of their kids these days. According to Nijole V. Benokraitis in <u>Marriages & Families: Changes, Choices and Contraints,</u> "Of the 187 participants at FORTUNE MAGAZINE'S MOST POWERFUL WOMEN IN BUSINESS SUMMIT, 1/3 of the women's husbands were stay-at-home dads."

Pro Card Two:

Quotations from book:

In the book it says "William wanted a doll...just as though he were its father and it were his child" (5 & 10).
"William's grandmother smiled. 'He needs it,' she said, 'to hug and to cradle and to take to the park so that when he's a father like you, he'll know how to take care of his baby and feed him and love him and bring him the things he wants, like a doll so that he can practice being a father" (30-32). The grandmother supports William's request by using the circle of life and the power of modeling to make a convincing argument in favor of William getting a doll. This supports my WTS because she is describing nurturing.

Josh repeated his strawman pattern believing his fact #5 canceled out argument #1 and as such refuted it. He said that his statistic I #3 nailed his thesis by adding a more positive reason—the stay-at-home dads. Further, he thought he'd use quotation #2 from the grandmother (yellow card) as his conclusion. He muttered, "I have to figure out a way to get from the fact to the statistic." Josh knew he needed a good transition.

Pattern **3**: Concession

This pattern begins much like strawman with the opposing argument or argument following the WTS but instead of knocking down the opposition, the writer concedes to its validity then offers an argument or several that support or defend the WTS.

While lawyers favor strawman, politicians favor concession. The strategy works best when there are opposing views that can neither be ignored nor refuted. The trick to making concession work is the transition from the opposing argument to the section that defends the WTS. Students learn to craft words and phrases that set up something contrary to what has just been proposed such as *contrary to . . ., but . . ., in contrast . . ., except . . ., although . . ., nevertheless . . .,* or *even so.*

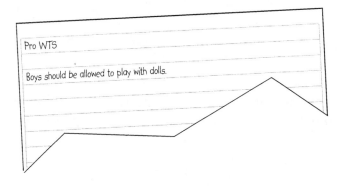

Josh followed his WTS with the expert testimony #3 from his CON cards (blue card), the notion that this behavior leads to perversion.

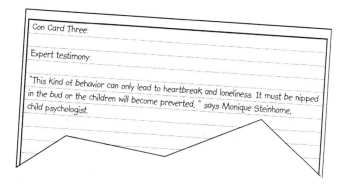

Then he used a transition—*in spite of this expert viewpoint from a professional psychologist*—to concede the validity of the opposition, but then he goes on to suggest that experience is a stronger argument, a stronger defense of his WTS. This segue leads to his anecdote: *My father is an expert, too. He lived with three sisters and is*

raising my two sisters and me. Here is his viewpoint. Then Josh offered #4 from his PRO cards (yellow), the full, actual anecdote.

Pro Card Four:

Anecdote:

I talked to my father. He said because he had three sisters, two older and one younger, he was surrounded by dolls. But there weren't any boys in his neighborhood, so he played with his sisters. "We had fun making up characters," he said. "I remember once we played <u>The Wizard of Oz</u>. My oldest sister picked Dorothy. The other older sister chose Glenda, the Good Witch. They let me play, so I pretended my doll was the Wicked Witch of the West. My kid sister got to play Toto." Then my father said, "Son, I don't think dolls are good or bad playthings; I think it matters what you do with them."

Josh said he was going to try for a contemplative ending with #5 about the action figures by giving "Something to get people thinking."

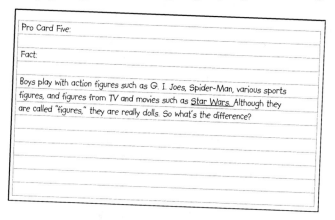

Pro Card Five:

Fact:

Boys play with action figures such as G. I. Joes, Spider-Man, various sports figures, and figures from TV and movies such as <u>Star Wars</u>. Although they are called "figures," they are really dolls. So what's the difference?

Pattern **4**: Nestorian Order

Our personal favorite pattern is Nestorian Order, perhaps because we together have read over eighty years of essays that began with a punch and then just ran dry or dwindled into oblivion, losing any point made earlier. These essays always reminded us of a couple of lines in "Out, Out," Robert Frost's poem:

> Little—less—nothing!—and that ended it.
> No more to build on there.

Nestorian Order takes care of that fading away through its unique pattern. The teacher models and then explains that in Nestorian Order the argument is developed by giving the second best reason first, then the minor reasons, finishing with the most powerful reason. This leaves the reader psychologically predisposed to the powerful argument because of the recency effect—the last thing read. Let's look at what Josh did with this pattern and his cards.

Josh really grappled with this pattern. He reordered his cards several times. We could almost see his thinking as he weighed his data. Finally he placed his cards in this order, mumbling, "I want to use them all."

Pro WTS

Boys should be allowed to play with dolls.

Pro Card Two:

Quotations from book:

In the book it says "William wanted a doll...just as though he were its father and it were his child" (5 & 10). "William's grandmother smiled. 'He needs it,' she said, 'to hug and to cradle and to take to the park so that when he's a father like you, he'll know how to take care of his baby and feed him and love him and bring him the things he wants, like a doll so that he can practice being a father" (30-32). The grandmother supports William's request by using the circle of life and the power of modeling to make a convincing argument in favor of William getting a doll. This supports my WTS because she is describing nurturing.

Pro Card One:

Argument in defense:

When boys play with dolls they learn how to nurture babies, a skill a boy will need when he has his own children.

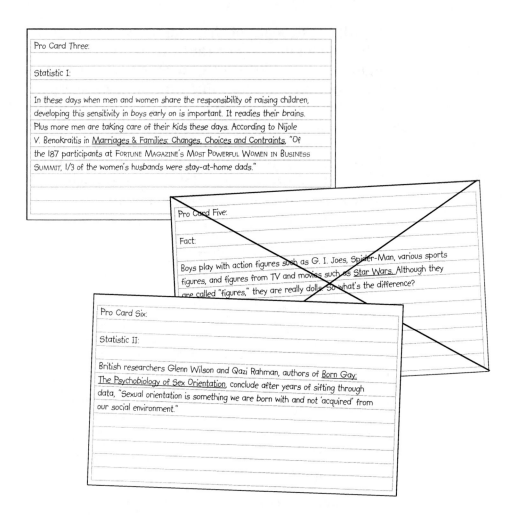

Pro Card Three:

Statistic I:

In these days when men and women share the responsibility of raising children, developing this sensitivity in boys early on is important. It readies their brains. Plus more men are taking care of their kids these days. According to Nijole V. Benokraitis in <u>Marriages & Families: Changes, Choices and Contraints</u>, "Of the 187 participants at Fortune Magazine's Most Powerful Women in Business Summit, 1/3 of the women's husbands were stay-at-home dads."

Pro Card Five:

Fact:

Boys play with action figures such as G. I. Joes, Spider-Man, various sports figures, and figures from TV and movies such as <u>Star Wars</u>. Although they are called "figures," they are really dolls. So what's the difference?

Pro Card Six:

Statistic II:

British researchers Glenn Wilson and Qazi Rahman, authors of <u>Born Gay: The Psychobiology of Sex Orientation</u>, conclude after years of sifting through data, "Sexual orientation is something we are born with and not 'acquired' from our social environment."

Josh maintained that the grandmother rationale in the book was second best because it set up the entire argument about how caring for a doll prepares boys for fatherhood through the actual words of the grandmother. He thought #1 was a restatement of the quotation just stated in his own words.

Josh explained that #3 supported the nurture argument with a statistic that was objective and quantitative about stay-at-home dads. He literally injected #5 because, "I want to use all my cards."

Josh liked #6 as his power punch because it made the point that environment does not make boys sissies.

Determined to use all his cards, Josh said #4, the anecdote about this father, would once again make a great conclusion as a clincher, but he wisely dropped #5 about the action figures because he realized, "I just can't make it fit."

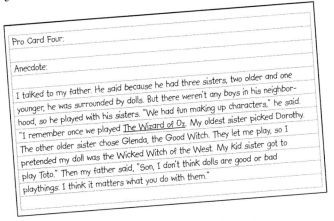

Pro Card Four:

Anecdote:

I talked to my father. He said because he had three sisters, two older and one younger, he was surrounded by dolls. But there weren't any boys in his neighborhood, so he played with his sisters. "We had fun making up characters," he said. "I remember once we played The Wizard of Oz. My oldest sister picked Dorothy. The other older sister chose Glenda, the Good Witch. They let me play, so I pretended my doll was the Wicked Witch of the West. My kid sister got to play Toto." Then my father said, "Son, I don't think dolls are good or bad playthings; I think it matters what you do with them."

At this point in the process, each student makes a commitment to his or her thesis. They rework for precision. No longer will they be working with the WTS but with their FTS (final thesis statement). Josh modified his to read: *Little boys should be allowed to play with dolls.* He explained, "Without the word *little*, people might misunderstand my rhetorical stance."

DAYS THIRTEEN and FOURTEEN

Students assemble their compositions, revise, conference, peer edit (clocking), and put the finishing touches on their papers.

The point is not whether the teacher agrees or disagrees with the WTS/FTS or the arguments, the point is whether the student ably follows a pattern in a coherent, unified way to support the WTS/FTS. Some patterns work better for some students' research, which underscores our mantra that meaning dictates form—**not** the other way around. The student who brilliantly pulls off equal arguments arguing PRO is as entitled to the high grade as is the student using the same pattern but arguing CON. As we say in Chapter 1, Aristotle insisted that while rational discourse should be enough to persuade someone, he believed that "It is not sufficient to know what one ought to say, but one must also know how to say it." These patterns enable that level of choice.

APPENDIX

A SUGGESTED MNEMONIC DEVICE FOR STUDENTS TO REMEMBER THE MAJOR RHETORICIANS OR A QUICK GUIDE FOR DEBATERS

The brain engages in acts of association all the time. Give a group of people a word, for example *football*, and ask them to say the first thing that pops into their heads. Different people say different things ranging from *I was a cheerleader, the band, getting my buns sore sitting in the stands, hot chocolate, King and Queen,* to *receiving my letter jacket,* and so on.

When we study persuasion, that important arm of rhetoric, we often get the various thinkers confused. The memory jogger below, based on that feat of association our brains naturally make, provides a word or two that will open up the students' long-term memory and allow all the details connected to that rhetorician to flood their minds and influence their writing.

Our intention here is to provoke an association between thinker and theory that triggers what students know and allows them to expand on that knowing and to use it appropriately.

This list is *not* meant to oversimplify the great minds represented here; rather it is meant as a mnemonic tool for students.

When you hear:	think:
Plato	truth
Aristotle	intent
The Sophists	power
Cicero	probability
Quintilian	credibility
Pavlov	conditioning
Freud	unconscious
Rogers	self-realization
Burke	motive
Young, Becker, and Pike	physics
Toulmin	rational process

After students have internalized this mnemonic, remind them to call upon this when taking tests such as the AP test in both English and U.S. history.

APPENDIX B

REGISTERS OF LANGUAGE DEFINED

Martin Joos in *The Five Clocks* describes five registers:

- **Frozen:** Unchanging language such as the U.S. Constitution, the Pledge of Allegiance, biblical passages. This language is literally frozen, "I pledge."
- **Formal:** While this includes introductions between people, it is primarily technical vocabulary. Usually it is a one-way communication such as a lecture, "Listen to me."
- **Consultative:** Think teacher/student, doctor/patient, expert/ apprentice. This includes academic conversation. This two-way communication often includes interruptive comments such "uh huh," "I see."
- **Casual:** The communication of friends and acquaintances, "Hi! What's going on?"
- **Intimate:** Private communications among family and close friends. This sometimes includes private vocabulary and allusions, "I wuv you."

M. A. K. Halliday, Angus McIntosh, and Peter Strevens, *The Linguistic Sciences and Language Teaching*, offer these registers:

- **Instrumental:** This is language used to get things done, for satisfying material needs, "I want."
- **Regulatory:** This language controls the behavior, feelings, and attitudes of others, "Do as I tell you."
- **Interactional:** Language used to establish status or to get along with others, "Me and you; me against you."
- **Personal:** This language expresses individuality or awareness of self, "Here I come."
- **Heuristic:** Language used to seek information or test knowledge, "Tell me why."
- **Imaginative:** Language used to create, "Let's pretend."
- **Representational:** This language communicates, "I've got something to tell you."

Frank Smith, "The Uses of Language," *Language Arts* 54, no. 6, adds:

- **Divertive:** Language used for fun, e.g. riddles, puns, etc., "Enjoy this."
- **Contractual:** This is the language used in contracts, "How it must be."
- **Perpetuating:** This language preserves, "How it was."

In a speech "Relating Reading and Writing," delivered at the 32nd Conference on College Composition and Communication in Dallas, Texas, Yetta Goodman suggested:

- **Ritualistic:** The everyday language we use to get along with others, "How are you?" This is sometimes called "phatic."
- **Extending memory:** Language used by authority to test knowledge—the language of tests, "Here is what I want to know."

APPENDIX

PERSUASIVE
THESES

The FBI's terrorist hunt is a failure.

Consumers are at a disadvantage in health care.

The government should require more testing and evaluation of the chemicals children are exposed to daily.

The mouthpieces of band instruments should be sanitized after each use because they carry a number of types of bacteria, including staph.

I am sick and tired of America's nitwit Anglophiles.

Many don't realize that tomatoes are a fruit.

I support the National Disaster Search Dog Foundation.

You are what you owe.

The government needs to investigate "for-profit" colleges.

I want to persuade you that Alexander McQueen, the British fashion designer who took his own life in February 2010, should not be featured at this year's Costume Institute exhibition at New York City's Metropolitan Museum of Art.

I think "Shark Week" on the Discovery Channel is stupid.

Emma Watson is my hero.

A Visit from the Goon Squad deserved to win the Pulitzer Prize.

Five years after you quit smoking, your risk of stroke is the same as someone who's never smoked.

Food is the biggest weapon in the world's fight for peace.

Prince William and Kate Middleton's wedding was my version of a fairy tale.

The King James Bible was not a book of poetry or philosophy or music or mystery but something of all these, which is one reason its rhythms remain embedded in our language 400 years after its publication on May 2, 1611.

The singers on *American Idol* need to hear the ugly truth.

Do you think there is too much political carping on TV?

Bullying pushes everyone's buttons these days.

What is your stand on free will?

Teachers should not take the blame for political blunders.

Human trafficking is more similar in America and Cambodia than we would like to admit.

Is loyalty dead?

APPENDIX

THE MAJOR FALLACIES

Students sometimes create fallacious arguments in their zeal to make their point or win the argument. Over the years we have tabulated the following as the most common major fallacies committed by students. (Many more fallacies may be found on the Internet.)

AD HOMINEM

Ad hominem comes from the Latin meaning "to the man." It's an abbreviation for *argumentum ad hominem*, which simply tries to link the truth of the thesis to a negative characteristic of a person. This fallacy is really a personal attack.

> Ex: Mr. Bradley is an uneducated buffoon with a big mouth. No one believes him when he says that thinking is gobbledygook.

BANDWAGON

Joyce came home once with a C grade on a paper. Because this was unusual, her mother questioned her. "Everyone got low grades; it was a bad test," claimed Joyce. To which her mother answered, "If everyone jumped off the bridge, would you? I don't care about 'everyone,' I want to know if you did your best." Joyce employed the fallacy of arguing because "everyone" did poorly it excused her low grade. She used bandwagon, and Mother didn't buy it.

> Ex: Everybody wears baggy jeans, so if you want to belong, you should wear them, too.

BEGGING THE QUESTION

We like to call this "assumicide" because either the thesis statement, which needs to be proven or defended, is assumed true or it is repeated in different words and becomes a form of circular reasoning. Its name comes from the idea of "begging" the listener to accept the thesis before the labor of logic is undertaken.

> Ex: So what if french fries are bad for you, adding extra calories to your diet. Eating fries—cholesterol and all—is part of being a kid.

POST HOC OR POST HOC PROPTER HOC

This fallacy rides on coincidence and as such serves superstition: If something happens when something else happens, the fault in logic is that the one caused the other. When something comes at the same time or just after something else, this classic fallacy holds that the first thing caused the second.

> Ex: For every basketball game I wear the same socks I wore during our winning game. I even put them on the same way. They bring me good luck.

TESTIMONIAL

This fallacy is tricky. Students often are unable to distinguish between a well-known, respected person who is credible in a particular field and someone who is well known and respected in some other field. So if a rock star endorses pizza, it is not the same as if an Iron Chef endorses it. When it comes to academic subjects, this becomes even more difficult for the neophyte.

> Ex: Selina Gomez says, "I eat wheat-bits to sing better. If you want to be a singer, you should eat wheat-bits, too."

THE HALF TRUTH

The half-truth or "sin of omission" is a favorite of kids because while they are telling some truth, they are also leaving out part of the truth—the important key details. Kids may tell their parents about an impending party at their friend's house but omit the important detail that the friend's parents will not be home. This incomplete information leads to false conclusions.

> Ex: The cheerleaders are leaders in our school.

REFERENCES

Aristotle. *The Rhetoric of Aristotle Book III.* E. M. Sandys and John Edwin (eds.). Cambridge: Cambridge University Press, 1877.

Aristotle. *Prior Analytics.* Trans. Robin Smith. Indianapolis, IN: Hackett Publishing, 1989.

Babbitt, Natalie. *Tuck Everlasting.* New York: Farrar, Straus and Giroux, 1975.

Benokraitis, Nijole V. *Marriages & Families: Changes, Choices and Constraints.* Upper Saddle River, NJ: Prentice Hall, 2010.

Bridges, Shirin Yim. *Ruby's Wish.* San Francisco, CA: Chronicle Books, 2002.

Bruffee, Kenneth A. *A Short Course in Writing.* Cambridge: Winthrop Publishers, 1972.

Burke, Kenneth. *A Grammar of Motives.* Berkeley, CA: University of California Press, 1969.

Carroll, Joyce Armstrong. *Conclusions: The Unicorns of Composition.* Spring, TX: Absey, 2004.

Carroll, Joyce Armstrong, and Edward E. Wilson. *Acts of Teaching: How to Teach Writing* (2nd ed.). Westport, CT: Teacher Ideas Press, 2008.

Cherry, Lynne. *The Great Kapok Tree.* New York: Sandpiper, 2000.

Cicero, Marcus Tullius. *De Inventione.* Whitefish, MT: Kessinger Publishers.

Cronin, Doreen. *Click, Clack, Moo: Cows That Type.* New York: Simon & Schuster, 2000.

Czech, Kenneth P. *Snapshot: America Discovers the Camera.* Minneapolis, MN: Lerner Publications, 1996.

Frost, Robert. "Out—Out . . ." In *Poetry After Lunch: Poems to Read Aloud.* Joyce Armstrong Carroll and Edward E. Wilson (eds.). Spring, TX: Absey, 1997.

Glass, Lillian. *Toxic People.* New York: St. Martin's Griffin, 1995.

Halliday, M. A. K. *Language as Social Semiotic: The Social Interpretation of Language and Meaning.* London: Edward Arnold, 1978.

Henkes, Kevin. *Owen.* New York: Greenwillow Books, 1993.

Hillocks, George, Jr. "Teaching Argument for Critical Thinking and Writing: An Introduction." *English Journal* 99, no. 6 (July 2010): 24–32.

Joos, Martin. *The Five Clocks.* New York: Harcourt, Brace and World, 1961.

Joseph, Sister Miriam. *The Trivium: The Liberal Arts of Logic, Grammar, and Rhetoric.* Philadelphia, PA: Paul Dry Books, 2002.

Krull, Kathleen, and Paul Brewer. *Lincoln Tells a Joke: How Laughter Saved the President (and the Country).* New York: Harcourt Children's Books, 2005.

Leibovich, Mark. "Being Glenn Beck." *New York Times Magazine* (Oct. 3, 2010), MM34.

Neeld, Elizabeth Cowan. *Writing* (2nd ed.). Glenview, IL: Scott, Foresman, 1980.

Orloff, Karen Kaufman. *I Wanna Iguana.* New York: Putnam's Sons, 2004.

Rappaport, Doreen. *Martin's Big Words: The Life of Dr. Martin Luther King, Jr.* New York: Hyperion, 2001.

Rylant, Cynthia. *The Ticky-Tacky Doll.* New York: Harcourt, 2002.

Sanderson, Brandon. *Mistborn.* New York: Tom Doherty Associates Book, 2006.

Skurzynski, Gloria. *Spider's Voice.* New York: Simon Pulse, 2001.

Smith, Frank. "The Uses of Language." *Language Arts* 54, no. 6, 1980.

Sorensen, Theodore C. *Kennedy.* Old Saybrook, CT: Konecky and Konecky, 1965.

Toulmin, Stephen. *The Uses of Argument.* Cambridge: Cambridge University Press, 1969.

Viorst, Judith. *Earrings!* New York: Atheneum, 2010.

Watt, Mélanie. *Have I Got a Book for You!* Toronto, Canada: Kids Can Press, 2009.

Willems, Mo. *Don't Let the Pigeon Drive the Bus.* New York: Hyperion Press, 2003.

Young, Richard E., Alton L. Becker, and Kenneth L. Pike. *Rhetoric: Discovery and Change.* New York: Harcourt, Brace & World, 1970.

Zolotow, Charlotte. *William's Doll.* New York: HarperTrophy, 1985.

INDEX

ABOUT THE AUTHORS

JOYCE ARMSTRONG CARROLL, EdD, HLD, has taught every grade level in her fifty-three years of teaching. She was professor of English and writing at McMurry University and is codirector of Abydos Learning International, formerly the New Jersey Writing Project in Texas (NJWPT), with her husband, Edward E. Wilson. Carroll has served as president of the Texas Council of Teachers of English Language Arts, served on the National Council of Teachers of English's Commission on Composition, and was chair of NCTEs Standing Committee Against Censorship. She has written over sixteen books for teachers such as *Acts of Teaching: How to Teach Writing*, *Dr. JAC's Guide to Writing with Depth*, *Authentic Strategies for High-Stakes Tests*, *Brushing Up on Grammar*, and *Phonics Friendly Books* plus hundreds of journal articles. Carroll coauthored with her husband Prentice Hall's *Writing and Grammar Series 6–12*.

EDWARD E. WILSON is codirector of Abydos Learning International, formerly the New Jersey Writing Project in Texas (NJWPT), with his wife, Joyce Armstrong Carroll. Wilson has taught on the elementary, secondary, and junior college levels and is a member of NCTE, TCTELA, CREST, and ASCD. A poet, he coedited *Poetry After Lunch* with Carroll and coauthored with her *Acts of Teaching*, *Brushing Up on Grammar*, and Prentice Hall's *Writing and Grammar Series 6–12*. Wilson is also the owner of Absey & Co., and is a publisher committed to educational excellence and creative works of literary merit.

CPSIA information can be obtained
at www.ICGtesting.com
Printed in the USA
FFOW01n1810140815
15979FF

9 781598 849509